Tapestries and Textiles

Louise Spilsbury

PowerKiDS
press.

New York

What are tapestries and textiles?

Tapestry and textile art is made using fabrics and fibers. Sometimes, textile art is purely **decorative**, such as wall hangings that are used instead of paintings. Some textile art is **functional**, such as blankets that are made to keep people warm. Some forms of textile art are both functional and decorative!

Tapestries

Tapestries are woven pictures. **Weaving** is an ancient skill that people developed as long ago as 6000 BC. Fragments of tapestries have even been found from ancient Egypt! The earliest known European tapestries are from the eleventh century. Throughout the **Middle Ages**, large tapestries were used to brighten up the huge, plain, stone walls of medieval castles. Whole rooms were often covered in a sequence of tapestries that worked together to tell a story.

▼ Many tapestries from the Middle Ages show Bible stories or scenes of everyday life, such as hunting. Rich people took their tapestries from house to house with them, to make rooms look cosy and to show off the family's wealth.

▶ The Hmong people lived in China and then Vietnam, but were attacked and chased out of this country. They often had to swim to safety in nearby Thailand. This twentieth-century, appliquéd cloth tells the story of the Hmong people's escape to freedom.

Textile art

Other kinds of textile art include **embroidery** and **appliqué**. Embroidery is when a piece of fabric is decorated with stitches of thread. In appliqué, fabric shapes are sewn or stuck onto a larger piece of fabric. These forms of textile art were first used when people lived a **nomadic** life, roaming from place to place. Women made decorative textiles, such as rugs, cushions, and blankets, because these items could be rolled up easily and carried with them. Then, when people set up camp somewhere new, the items were brought out again.

How to use this book

Background information on each tapestry or textile featured, including its designer, date, location, and history

This section tells you about the story behind each tapestry or textile

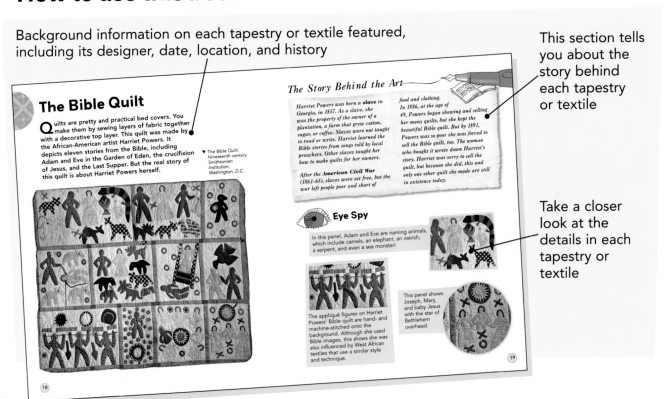

Take a closer look at the details in each tapestry or textile

The Bible Quilt

Quilts are pretty and practical bed covers. You make them by sewing layers of fabric together with a decorative top layer. This quilt was made by the African-American artist Harriet Powers. It depicts eleven stories from the Bible, including Adam and Eve in the Garden of Eden, the crucifixion of Jesus, and the Last Supper. But the real story of this quilt is about Harriet Powers herself.

▼ The Bible Quilt
Nineteenth century
Smithsonian Institution,
Washington, D.C.

The Story Behind the Art

Harriet Powers was born a slave in Georgia, in 1837. As a slave, she was the property of the owner of a plantation, a farm that grew cotton, sugar, or coffee. Slaves were not taught to read or write. Harriet learned the Bible stories from songs told by local preachers. Other slaves taught her how to make quilts for her owners.

After the American Civil War (1861–65), slaves were set free, but the war left people poor and short of food and clothing.
In 1886, at the age of 49, Powers began showing and selling her many quilts, but she kept the beautiful Bible quilt. But by 1891, Powers was so poor she was forced to sell the Bible quilt, too. The woman who bought it wrote down Harriet's story. Harriet was sorry to sell the quilt, but because she did, this and only one other quilt she made are still in existence today.

Eye Spy

In this panel, Adam and Eve are naming animals, which include camels, an elephant, an ostrich, a serpent, and even a sea monster!

The appliqué figures on Harriet Powers' Bible quilt are hand- and machine-stitched onto the background. Although she used Bible images, this shows she was also influenced by West African textiles that use a similar style and technique.

This panel shows Joseph, Mary, and baby Jesus with the star of Bethlehem overhead.

18

19

How are textiles made?

Different textiles are made in different ways. Some, such as silk painting, are simply paints applied to fabric. Other kinds of textiles are more complicated.

Making tapestries

Tapestries are designs made on a **loom**, a simple machine used to weave two or more threads together. On a loom, **warp** threads go down and then **weft** threads are woven left to right, in and out of the warp threads. The patterns in a tapestry are usually woven by the weft threads. For example, on a loom the warp threads are a neutral color. The weft threads, in different colors, are woven in and out of the warp threads in different sequences to make a pattern or a picture.

◄ *This Native American woman in Arizona is teaching her daughter to weave a rug. You can see the cream-colored vertical warp threads and the multicolored weft threads that form the pattern going horizontally (across) the loom.*

Appliqué

Appliqué is a French word that means to apply, or to put on. In appliqué, paper patterns are made and are used to cut small fabric shapes. These pieces are then sewn or stuck onto a larger piece of background fabric with the edges turned underneath. A number of different pieces are applied to form a picture or pattern. Often, other materials, such as beads and sequins, are sewn on the appliqué to create different effects and **textures**. Sometimes appliqué has embroidery on it, too.

Embroidery

In embroidery, different kinds of stitches are used to give different effects. Some stitches are used to make outlines, such as a running stitch, in which the needle is pulled under and over the fabric in regular spaces. Other stitches are used to fill an outline, such as satin stitch, in which lots of stitches of different lengths are made next to each other. Other stitches are simply decorative, such as the French knot, in which you wrap the thread to make a little knot on the fabric surface.

▼ *These bold-colored embroidery stitches are being used to decorate a skirt.*

The Lady and the Unicorn

This tapestry, called *Sight*, is one of a sequence about the Lady and the Unicorn. The Lady and the Unicorn tapestries were made for Jean Le Viste, a nobleman in the French court of King Charles VII during the Middle Ages.

▼ The Lady and the Unicorn: Sight
Fifteenth century
122 x 130 in.
(310 x 330 cm)
Museum of the Middle Ages, Paris, France

The Story Behind the Art

The story goes that in the Middle Ages, many hunters tried to capture the magical unicorn. They believed its horn cured fevers and stopped people from growing old. Unicorns were rarely seen because they lived deep within dark, mysterious forests. One day, a hunter saw a unicorn in the distance. He organized a group of men and dogs to chase it, but the unicorn always escaped.

As the unicorn ran from its pursuers, it came upon a beautiful young woman. The woman reached out and softly stroked its mane. The unicorn liked her gentle touch and was fascinated by its reflection in her mirror. It moved closer and laid its head on her lap. At this moment, the hunters made their move, and captured and killed the unicorn. The woman was deeply saddened by the death of the unicorn, but was later comforted when she saw its spirit in the forest.

 ## Eye Spy

Tapestries with lots of flowers decorating the background are known as millefleurs, which means "thousands of flowers." This style was characteristic of tapestries in the Middle Ages and was inspired by the custom of spreading cut flowers on roads and paths on festival days in those times.

Animals in the background of the tapestry are decorative, but are also **symbols** of families' hopes or beliefs. For example, the weasel represents courageous fighters and the rabbit represents having lots of children. The unicorn also represented Jesus for Christian believers.

The Le Viste family coat of arms appears on each piece of the Lady and the Unicorn tapestry. The crescent moons in the diagonal stripe may show that the family has been honored by royalty.

The Story of Buddha

This is a thangka from Tibet. A thangka is a **Buddhist** painting made on canvas and mounted on cotton or silk. Thangkas can be rolled up and carried between temples and villages for Buddhist festivals. Many thangkas tell stories from the life of **Buddha**.

◀ *Tibetan temple banner*
Eighteenth century
Musee Guimet, Paris,
France

The Story Behind the Art

The hero of this story is Siddhartha, a prince born over 2,500 years ago in the Himalayas. For many years, Siddhartha was unaware of what went on outside his palace. Then, at 29, he ventured beyond the palace walls and saw four people who changed his life: an old man, a sick man, a dead man, and a wandering holy man. Siddhartha was so moved by these people that he set out to find a way to stop the suffering in the world.

Siddhartha spent six years studying with many religious teachers. Then he sat under a tree in quiet meditation. He did this for 49 days, in spite of attacks from an evil spirit named Mara. Through this, he found enlightenment—he reached the great understanding that only when people stop wanting things and instead live a simple life can they be truly happy. At this moment, Siddhartha became Buddha, the Enlightened One, and the religion of Buddhism began.

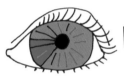 **Eye Spy**

On a thangka, the background color is put on first, then the figures and details are added. Traditional thangka colors are black, white, red, yellow, green, and blue. The design of a thangka is usually **symmetrical**, with the important central figure surrounded by less important ones.

Buddha sits cross-legged on a large lotus flower. In Buddhism, the lotus flower is a symbol of things that are good and pure. It means that Buddha is pure of mind and spirit.

As a sign of his new spiritual life, when he leaves home Siddhartha leaves behind his fancy clothes and his heavy gold earrings. This is why he is shown with long empty earlobes. He also cuts off his hair with his sword.

The Dragon Robe

This silk dragon robe was made for an empress, wife of the emperor of China. Only the emperor and his family wore robes with the five-toed dragon symbol, because it represented the emperor's great power.

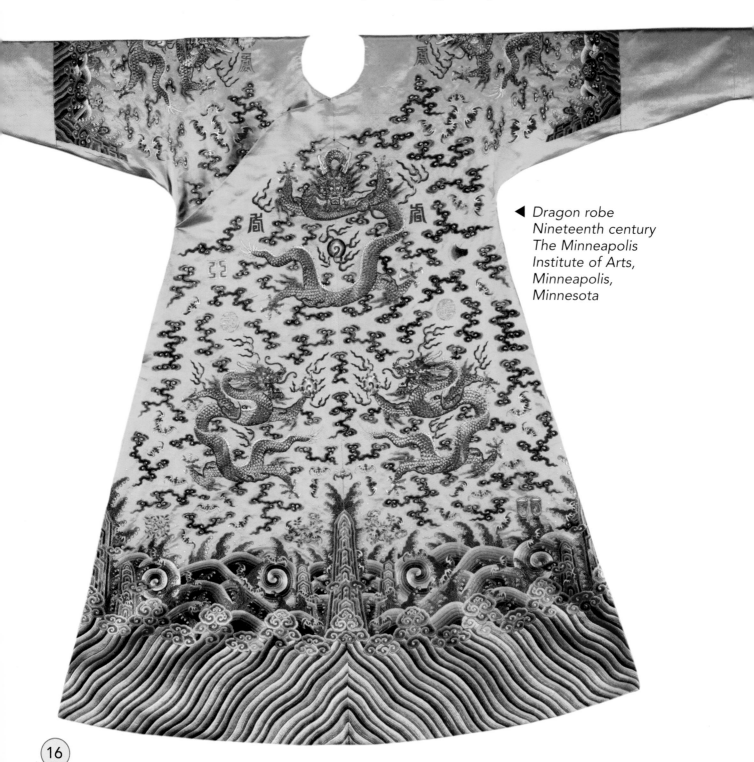

◀ Dragon robe
Nineteenth century
The Minneapolis
Institute of Arts,
Minneapolis,
Minnesota

The Story Behind the Art

Legend has it that, long ago, magical dragons lived in secret caves or at the bottom of the sea in China. The emperor sometimes called on a dragon to summon help from heaven. During the T'ang dynasty (618–907 AD), there was a terrible period of **drought**. With no rain, crops were dying and people were starving to death.

The emperor sent a messenger to ask an Indian priest, Wu Wei, to use his magical powers to call the dragon.

Wu Wei emptied his temple of everything except a bowl of water. Stirring it, he chanted magical words over and over again. A dragon appeared from the bowl. It wafted out of the temple door as white smoke. Instantly, a blanket of darkness fell over the earth, and thunder, lightning, and rain filled the sky. The messenger returned to court just in time to warn the emperor the storms were coming, as fierce winds blew giant trees into his path.

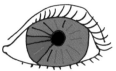 # Eye Spy

This image of the Chinese dragon shows it tossing a flaming pearl between its paws. The pearl was a symbol of the dragon's wisdom.

In China, bats are symbols of happiness, because the Chinese word for "bat" and "happiness" sound similar when you say them. The bats on this robe were meant to bring long life and happiness to the empress who wore it.

The mountain, clouds, and waves at the bottom of the robe are symbols of the belief that the emperor had the power to go between heaven and earth.

Fante Flags

The Fante are people who live along the coast of the country of Ghana in West Africa. The flags they make are bold and colorful, and are used to represent their family groups, a little like coats-of-arms. The images on the Fante flags are embroidered or appliquéd onto a large background cloth.

Asafo means "men of war." The original Fante flags were designed to insult enemies in battle or to boast of a group's skill or power. Today, Ghana is a more peaceful place than in the past, but Fante family groups still make these beautiful flags to show on festival days, funerals, and at other times when the community gets together.

▼ *Asafo company flag*
Kobina Badowa
1970
70 x 44 in.
(180 x 113 cm)
Fowler Museum, University of California, Los Angeles, CA

The Story Behind the Art

From the fifteenth century onward, European merchants used ports in Ghana to trade for gold, ivory, and slaves. Fante warriors were known as the Asafo. The Asafo worked with the Europeans, partly because doing so prevented attacks by their enemy, the Ashanti. There were over 300 separate family groups or companies of Asafo.

Asafo companies started to make flags like the European ones they saw, to represent their companies' strengths. Each company had a different design.

The designs show **proverbs** or sayings. They often use animals as symbols of power, for example, elephants and bulls represent strength, and crocodiles and cats illustrate hunting skills.

This flag shows the superiority of the Asafo company that owned it. The company members are warriors, shown on the right. Their enemies are pictured as vultures, birds that were considered offensive because they live off of dead meat waste that they find.

Eye Spy

This flag is the national flag of Ghana. Green, gold, and red are found on the national flags of many African nations and were used on many ancient African flags. The five-pointed star in the middle is a symbol of African people working together to gain independence from European countries that once ruled over them.

The rifles around the vultures' necks show that these birds are supposed to represent the Asafo company's rivals. These kinds of images were supposed to insult rivals.

EDƆMBIREB ΔΔNNΔ ʃΔΔ MPƐT ΔΔ

These words say "All our enemies are vultures" in Twi, one of the major languages spoken in Ghana. The words are written using Roman letters, and this reflects the Asafo people's interaction with Europeans.

Print a pattern

You will need:
piece of thick card or a wooden block • pen • glue • ball of string • fabric paint • piece of plain white or cream fabric, such as calico • roller or paintbrush

What you do:

1 Draw a simple design on the card or wooden block. Just draw the outline, you don't need to color it in. Maybe you could use nature for your inspiration; for example, you could draw the outline of a leaf shape.

2 Now, carefully paint glue over the lines of your outline and stick string over the pen lines. You have created a printing block.

3 Use a roller or paintbrush to apply fabric paint to the string. Then, press the printing block onto the piece of fabric.

4 Repeat to make an interesting pattern.

Top Tip!
You could make a piece of printed cloth large enough to make a cushion cover, purse, bag, or a curtain for a book corner!

Make a Fante flag

Think of a proverb or saying that could decorate a flag, or a symbol to represent your class—or illustrate a class event, such as a sports day.

You will need:
felt • glue
• needles and
thread • paper
• safety scissors
• sequins and
beads • pins

1 Draw your design on paper. Cut out the sections of the paper to make the pattern.

2 Pin the paper pattern pieces on the pieces of bright-colored felt. Then carefully cut out the felt around the pattern pieces.

3 Sew or glue extra pieces of fabric or sequins and beads on the felt for decoration. You could also add some decorative stitching to add details to your patterns.

4 Fix the finished felt designs to a big felt or fabric flag or banner, using a running stitch (see page 25) or glue.

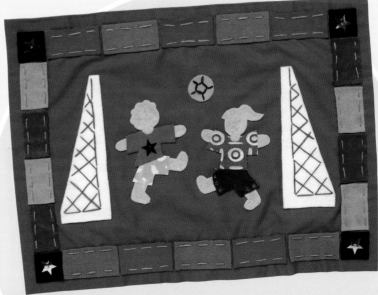

Weave your own tapestry

Make a loom and weave your own simple tapestry.

You will need: sturdy box, e.g. shoebox • ruler • pen • safety scissors • collection of different-colored yarn • tape • fork

1 Remove the lid from the shoebox and using a ruler and pen, make marks at $1/2$ in. (1 cm) intervals along opposite sides of the top of the box. Cut slits approximately $1/4$ in. (0.5 cm) long at each of the marking.

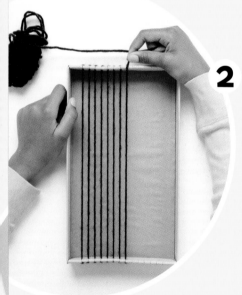

2 Now start making the warp (lengthwise threads). Fix the loose end of the yarn ball to the side of the box with a piece of tape. Then wrap the yarn (your warp thread) around the box, passing it through the slits at the top of the box and pulling the warp threads tight each time.

3 When you have lines of yarn across the whole box top, cut the yarn and stick the end of it to the box with more tape. This is your loom.

4 Now you're ready to start weaving. Take a long piece of colored yarn and tie one end to the warp thread on the bottom left-hand side of the box. Working from left to right, pull the loose end of this yarn under the first warp string, then over the second string. Weave under the following string, then over the next. Repeat this until you have woven across all the strings.

5 Now turn and make the second row of your tapestry by weaving in the opposite direction. It's important to make sure that you go over the yarn strings you went under on the first row, and under the strings you went over.

Top Tip!
Be careful not to pull the yarn too loose or too tight when turning the low end. After each row of weft threading, use your finger or a fork to pull the weft row into a straight, neat line across the loom.

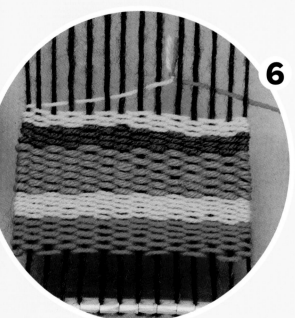

6 To change colors, simply tie the new color yarn to the end of the old color yarn, and push the knot into the back of the weaving so it won't show. You can change colors at the end of a row or in the middle.

7 When you have finished your tapestry, cut the warp threads as close to the edge of the box as you can. You can tie these together in pairs to create a tasseled effect, if you like.

Glossary

American Civil War   War between the North and South of the United States, partly about whether or not slavery should be abolished.

appliqué   Cut-out decoration sewn to a larger piece of material.

Buddha   Means "Enlightened One." Buddha is the founder of the religion of Buddhism.

Buddhist   Relating to the Buddhist religion.

decorative   Describes something that looks attractive rather than serves any useful purpose.

drought   An unusually long period with little or no rainfall.

embroidery   Decorating fabric or other materials by stitching strands of thread or yarn with a needle.

functional   Describes something useful.

invasion   When an army enters another country in order to conquer and take control of that country.

loom   Machine used for weaving yarn into a textile, such as a rug or blanket.

Middle Ages   European period of history between 500 and 1500 AD, sometimes called the Medieval times.

nomadic   Type of people with no permanent home. They frequently move from one location to another in search of food.

proverb   A short saying that gives advice or tells a truth about human behavior in an easy-to-remember form.

slave   Person who is owned by someone else and has to work for them without pay.

symbol   Something that stands for or represents something else.

symmetrical   Having each side the same. For example, the two sides of our faces are usually symmetrical.

texture   The feel or appearance of a material, for example, smooth or rough.

warp   The yarn or thread that goes vertically (lengthwise) on a loom.

weaving   Making textiles by interlacing two or more sets of yarns together, usually on a loom.

weft   The yarn or thread that goes horizontally (widthwise) on a loom.

Find out more

Books to read

Art from Fabric by Gillian Chapman (Hodder Wayland, 2005)
Artists at Work: Textile Artists by Cheryl Jakab (Smart Apple Media, 2007)
Arts Alive: What Are Textiles? by Ruth Thomson (Sea to Sea, 2005)
Designer Appliqué (Mini Maestro series), (Top That Publishing, 2001)
Science Files: Textiles by Steve Parker (Heinemann Library, 2002)
World Crafts: Textiles by Meryl Doney (Franklin Watts, 2005)

Websites to visit

Due to the changing nature of Internet links, PowerKids Press has developed an online list of Web sites related to the subject of this book. This site is updated regularly. Please use this link to access this list:
www.powerkidslinks.com/sia/taptex

Places to go

At the Metropolitan Museum, New York, you can see a series of beautiful series of unicorn tapestries.

The Museum of the American Quilters' Society, Kentucky, has a wide display of new and antique quilts.

The National Museum of the American Indian (New York, Maryland and Washington) has a wonderful collection of Native American textiles and clothing.

The San Jose Museum of Quilts and Textiles, California, has a wide display of historical quilts and ethnic textiles.

Index

Photos or pictures are shown below in bold, **like this**.